Expense Report Best Practices

Steven M. Bragg

AccountingTools®

ISBN 978-1-64221-287-7

For more information about AccountingTools® products, visit our Web site at www.accountingtools.com.

Table of Contents

Expense Report Best Practices 1

Introduction *1*

Prohibited Expenditures *1*

Missing or Illegible Receipts *3*

Late Submissions *4*

Mileage Overstatements *5*

Excessive Tip Claims *5*

Card Misuse *5*

Cash Advances *6*

Forms of Documentation *7*

Online Expense Reporting *7*

Payables Department Review Practices *9*

Spend Management *9*

Dealing with Employee Departures *9*

Expense Report Audits *10*

The Escalation Process *11*

Training for First-Level Supervisors *12*

A Note Regarding Senior Management *12*

A Note Regarding Bureaucracy *12*

The Travel and Entertainment Policy *13*

Additional T&E Policies *15*

T&E Policy Updates *16*

Glossary **17**

Index **18**

About the Author

Steven Bragg, CPA, has been the chief financial officer or controller of four companies, as well as a consulting manager at Ernst & Young. He received a master's degree in finance from Bentley College, an MBA from Babson College, and a Bachelor's degree in Economics from the University of Maine. He has been a two-time president of the Colorado Mountain Club, and is an avid alpine skier, mountain biker, and certified master diver. Mr. Bragg resides in Centennial, Colorado. He has written more than 300 books and courses, including *New Controller Guidebook*, *GAAP Guidebook*, and *Payroll Management*.

Steven maintains the accountingtools.com web site, which contains continuing professional education courses, the Accounting Best Practices podcast, and thousands of articles on accounting subjects.

Buy Additional AccountingTools Courses

AccountingTools offers more than 1,500 hours of CPE courses, with concentrations in accounting, auditing, finance, taxation, and ethics. Related courses that you might like include:

- Optimal Accounting for Payables
- Payables Management
- Records Management

Go to accountingtools.com/cpe to view these additional courses.

AccountingTools®

Expense Report Best Practices

Introduction

Expense reports are submitted by employees in order to be reimbursed for expenses they incurred on behalf of the company. Expense reports are quite different from normal expenditures that originate in the purchasing department, since there is no authorizing purchase order or receiving report to document an expense. Expense reports primarily contain travel and entertainment (T&E) expenses, which can comprise a significant part of an organization's total expenditures. Given these issues, it is essential to maintain tight control over expense reports, but in a cost-effective manner. In this manual, we explore a number of best practices to maintain solid control over T&E expenditures, while avoiding an excessive amount of employee oversight.

> **Related Podcast Episodes:** Episodes 6 and 113 of the Accounting Best Practices Podcast discuss expense report controls and employee spend management systems, respectively. They are available at: **accountingtools.com/podcasts** or **iTunes**

Prohibited Expenditures

Employees may attempt to include prohibited items in their expense reports, such as the items noted in the following exhibit. These items can add up to substantial amounts, especially when management does not call out employees on these items – in which case employees become accustomed to charging these items through to their employer on a recurring basis. For example, a salesman might charge through the cost of child care while he is on a sales trip for the company, along with some incidental clothing while on the trip, gym fees while on the road, the occasional laundry fee, in-room movies, a magazine to read during flights, and a speeding ticket incurred while driving to a customer site.

It is usually not sufficient to rely on supervisors to review and approve the expense reports of their employees, because they give this task a low priority; instead, they generally do no more than glance at a report before approving it.

Sample List of Non-Reimbursement Items

Adult entertainment	Expenses > 90 days old	Personal reading material
Car washes and cleaning	Finance charges on credit cards	Theft/loss of personal property
Contributions	Health club / spa fees	Toiletries
Child care	Laundry fees on short-duration trips	Traffic fines
Clothing	Lost luggage	Travel insurance
Commuting costs	Movies	Undocumented expenses

A basic remediation step is to create a travel policy that specifically identifies all non-reimbursable items, ensure that employees are repeatedly forewarned about them, and then search for them during periodic audits. Auditors conduct much more detailed reviews of expense reports than supervisors. Whenever non-reimbursement items are spotted on an expense report, one should send a note to the offending employee, noting the problem and showing the applicable section of the corporate T&E policy that was breached. This is a good way to train employees in regard to what is considered an acceptable reimbursement item, which should reduce the number of issues in the future.

Best Practice: Create a standard form (either on paper or for electronic transmission) for issuing notices to employees about non-reimbursement items. Doing so reduces the cost of issuing these notices.

The same training approach can be used with any supervisor who approved a non-reimbursement item. Point out the item to the supervisor, making note of the relevant prohibition in the corporate travel policy, and discuss why the item was approved. In cases where the supervisor continues to approve non-reimbursement items, it may make sense to bring up the matter with a more senior level of management.

Best practice: Include the list of non-reimbursable items on the back of all expense report forms, so there can be no question about what they are.

Best practice: When non-reimbursement items are spotted on an expense report, notify the internal audit department. They will then give a higher priority to examining the expense reports of the employee who submitted the report.

Best practice: Once a non-reimbursable item has been spotted during an audit, have the auditor go back through that employee's expense reports for the last few years to see if there have been problems in prior periods. Doing so focuses audits on those employees who have a track record of breaking the rules.

> **Best practice:** When a manager insists on approving a non-reimbursement item on an employee expense report, consider breaking it out on the departmental income statement as a separate line item, so that the manager understands the total cost of these approvals over time.

An interesting approach to increase the cost of including non-reimbursable items on an expense report is to return these reports to employees with a request to re-submit the report without the questionable item. Doing so adds a few days to the reimbursement process, thereby increasing the cost to the employee – especially if he or she needs the cash to pay a personal credit card bill.

Another way to increase the cost for the employee is to request more extensive documentation of non-reimbursable items. Again, the point is to make it more difficult for the employee, who will be less inclined to submit these items in the future.

> **Best practice:** Include verbiage in the corporate T&E policy that repeated submissions of non-reimbursable items makes an employee more likely to be subject to an audit by the internal audit team.

Missing or Illegible Receipts

A problem that routinely causes trouble in the payables department is missing receipts or receipts that are illegible. When a person is intent on submitting a fraudulent expense report, they may deliberately submit receipts that are difficult to read, with the complaint of "what can you do?" when asked for a better copy. This can be combatted by stating in the company T&E policy that all receipts must be legible, thereby giving the payables staff an excellent excuse to deny expense report claims.

> **Best practice:** Set a minimum threshold for the receipts requirement, so that the payables staff and employees are not wasting time looking for the receipts for inconsequential amounts. This does mean that some fraudulent expenses will be reimbursed, but they will not cost much in aggregate.

A hard cutoff point for the preceding best practice is to mandate a receipt for every claimed expense of $75 or more. The reason is that, in Section 1.274-5(c)(2)(iii) of the Code of Federal Regulations, the IRS mandates the following:

> "…documentary evidence is required for (1) any expenditure for lodging while traveling away from home, and (2) any other expenditure of $75 or more except, for transportation charges, documentary evidence will not be required if not readily available."

Best practice: Require employees to submit a missing receipt affidavit, stating why a receipt is missing, and confirming that the receipt will not be used for a separate reimbursement request. Also require a supervisor's signature on the affidavit. The intent is to make the process annoying enough that employees will be more careful to retain receipts in the future.

Best practice: Maintain a listing of lost receipts by employee. When this happens too much with a particular person, give them advance warning that no further missing receipts will be reimbursed. This warning is intended to alter their behavior, and not to save the company money on un-reimbursed receipts.

Best practice: Require a detailed receipt for all meals. By doing so, one can spot improper expenditures, such as unusually expensive purchases, excess liquor purchases, takeout meals purchased for an employee's family, and so forth.

Late Submissions

Some employees have a terrible time submitting their expense reports in a timely manner. No matter how many times they are warned, they are simply unable to block out the time to collect their receipts and document them in an expense report. This may be because they assign expense reports an extremely low priority, and so would rather work on other tasks. Or, they may have an aversion to paperwork. In either case, dealing with these people is endlessly frustrating. In many cases, it does not seem to help when supervisors are brought in to issue stern warnings to the offending parties.

The obvious remediation step is to set a monthly date by which expense reports must be submitted, and broadcast the date a few days in advance to anyone likely to submit a report (such as the sales staff). However, this is rarely sufficient for the truly hard-core non-compliance employees. The following best practices may be of assistance.

Best practice: Shift the expense report preparation task over to a department secretary, with instructions to notify the department manager if the person for whom this work is being done is not cooperating. This approach puts the expense reporting function in the hands of someone who is hopefully more interested in completing the report on time.

Best practice: Have the accounting department issue an inter-departmental charge to any department whose employees submit expense reports late, and have this charge count against the performance criteria in the department manager's annual performance plan.

Best practice: Give the offending employee advance notice that no further travel advances will be issued until all missing expense reports have been submitted. This approach only works if the employee is actually in need of a travel advance, which is usually not the case for the more senior (and presumably better paid) employees.

Mileage Overstatements

It is quite time-consuming to evaluate the amount of mileage claimed by an employee for reimbursement on an expense report. The best approach is to reserve any reviews for cases in which mileage claims appear to be egregious, and only then conduct a detailed analysis of miles traveled. Another approach is to mandate the use of a detailed mileage log in cases where claims appear to be too high, and then analyze the individual line items for reasonableness. Given the high mileage rates at which employees are reimbursed, this can be worth the effort when large claims are involved. However, when the mileage claims are minimal, it is not worth the effort.

Best practice: If the company has common travel destinations, such as from the company headquarters to specific customers or suppliers, create a table that lists the miles that will be reimbursed for these standard trips, and issue it to employees. Be sure to update it as customers and suppliers change over time.

Excessive Tip Claims

Employees may claim excessively large tips given to service providers. These tips may be justified in cases of great service, but in other cases they are simply padding inserted into an expense report. A business can mitigate this issue by noting in the corporate T&E policy that tips will be reimbursed up to a certain cap, such as 20% of a meal.

Card Misuse

One of the more efficient ways to make purchases is with a corporate purchasing card, since it avoids the many steps involved in the purchasing and accounts payable processes. However, there is a significant probability that some employees will mis-use the purchasing cards that have been assigned to them. Common problems are:

- *Avoidance of purchasing cap.* An employee may attempt to avoid the maximum purchasing card threshold by having a supplier break down a large purchase into several smaller ones.
- *Personal purchases.* An employee may include small personal purchases on the purchasing card, so that the company pays for them.
- *Excessive purchases.* An employee may buy necessary items, but in quantities larger than is realistically needed over the near term.

The obvious starting point for how to deal with these problems is to develop a standard policy for the use of purchasing cards, on which is noted exactly how the cards are supposed to be used – and clarifying how they should *not* be used. The policy should also clearly state what will happen to any employees who circumvent the policy, which includes termination of employment.

A reasonable control point is for the responsible department manager to review and approve all purchasing card statements. In reality, they are typically in a rush and so do not engage in the type of detailed analysis that can spot improper purchases. A good backup option is to have someone in the accounts payable department conduct a separate review; if any unusual items are spotted, the payables manager can take them to the department manager for a more detailed discussion.

> **Best practice:** Have a human resources person discuss the purchasing card policy with each authorized card user, going through every part of the policy. Doing so ensures absolute clarity about card usage and the penalties for incorrect usage. Then have each user sign the policy to acknowledge receipt, and keep the signed copy on file. This takes away any possible defense that they did not know about the policy.

Despite the preceding issues, the use of corporate purchasing cards is highly recommended, since they avoid the game-playing that can arise from the use of personal credit cards. For example, an employee pays for a $500 training class at the local community college with her own credit card and includes this charge on her expense report as a valid training reimbursement. The company pays her $500, after which she cancels the class and obtains a refund from the community college through her credit card. If the company had instead mandated the use of a corporate purchasing card, this fraud situation could not have occurred.

An additional reason for eliminating personal credit cards is that employees will no longer be able to run their annual card fees through an expense report for reimbursement. Depending on the type of credit card, these annual fees can be substantial.

> **Best practice:** Funnel all applicable purchases through corporate purchasing cards, rather than cards owned by employees. Doing so gives the company better control over the purchases being made, and avoids any arguments about reimbursing employees for purchases they made on behalf of the company.

Cash Advances

A business may find it necessary to issue a cash advance to an employee in order to fund expenditures made during a business trip. The employee is then supposed to deduct the amount of the advance from the expense report resulting from the trip. The trouble is that many employees forget to deduct the advance, resulting in essentially a double payment to them when the company reimburses them for their submitted expense reports.

The traditional approach to this issue has been for the payables staff to manually track all cash advances made, so that they can be deducted from any expense reports submitted thereafter. This approach is time-consuming and subject to error. An alternative approach is to have the company directly pay for a larger proportion of travel costs through a corporate purchasing card, leaving fewer expenses that an employee will likely need to pay for. This step will not completely eliminate the need for cash advances, since some employees have so little cash on hand that they simply cannot support any part of a trip's projected costs.

An additional concern involving cash advances is that an employee may leave the company without ever having paid back an advance. This situation may not be spotted for months, since the payables staff is not usually notified of the departure of employees. One way to avoid this problem is to minimize the use of cash advances, or to have a policy that all advances must be repaid within one month. Another option is to include a notation on the employee termination form, reminding the human resources staff to check with the payables department to see if any cash advances are outstanding; if so, the remaining balance can be deducted from the employee's final paycheck.

Forms of Documentation

Do employees really need to attach the physical receipts to an expense report for all purchases made? This commonly results in a thick document package that takes up inordinate space in the payables files, and which is likely to fall apart. Also, providing paper-based proof of expenditures means that someone working off-site must mail in this documentation, and so must wait for the mail to be delivered before he or she can expect to receive a payment; this delay can be a real problem if an employee has a short deadline by which a credit card payment must be made.

A possible solution is to allow employees to scan their supporting documents and e-mail them to the payables department, along with a scanned version of the expense report. Doing so eliminates the mail float problem, while also making it optional for the payables staff to print out the receipts or store them electronically.

> **Best practice:** If the decision is made to require employees to submit paper receipts, have them tape these documents to a standard-size sheet of paper. Doing so makes it less likely that small-size receipts will be inadvertently detached from an expense report package.

Online Expense Reporting

Some companies require their employees to use an on-line form to submit their expense reports. This is an efficient way to record and review expenses, since the form typically incorporates the company's travel policy, which automatically rejects any submissions that are not in compliance with the policy. The procedure for completing an on-line expense report form is as follows:

1. *Enter information in system.* The on-line form prompts the employee to enter the dates and amounts of expenditures, as well as classify them into different expense categories. The system reviews these submissions based on the

corporate travel policy and automatically rejects those items prohibited by the policy.

2. *Enter receipts.* The system reviews the expenses submitted and decides which receipts should accompany them. Employees may have the option of scanning in the required receipts, or of mailing them to the payables department.

3. *Obtain approval.* The system routes a digital image of the expense report to the person designated as the supervisor of the employee. The supervisor reviews and approves the document, after which the system routes it to the payables department.

4. *Import expense report.* There should be an interface between the expense reporting system and the accounts payable system, so that expense report submissions are automatically set up for payment. The on-line form automatically assigns a unique number when an expense report has been submitted, which becomes the invoice number associated with that expense report.

The following exhibit shows a streamlined view of the on-line expense reporting procedure.

On-line Expense Reporting Process Flow

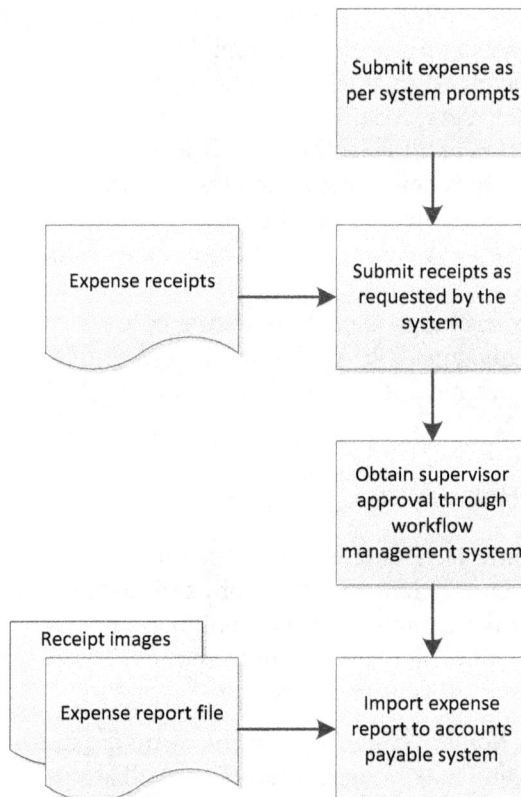

> **Best Practice:** Online expense reporting is a clearly superior approach, since the system automatically reviews entries as they are made into the system. However, developing such a system in-house is expensive, so we recommend using one of the many vendors who offer Internet-based expense reporting systems, such as SAP Concur, Nexonia, and Certify.

Payables Department Review Practices

The payables staff is responsible for conducting a review of all submitted expense reports, comparing claimed amounts to the corporate T&E policy and verifying that the numbers entered into each report add up to the claimed totals. In addition, they should compare all expense reports to a list of outstanding employee travel advances, to see if the advances were properly deducted from the expense reports. This is frequently not the case, where employees have conveniently forgotten to make the deduction. If so, the payables staff issues a notice to the employee and the person's supervisor regarding the amount of the deduction and how much will actually be reimbursed.

> **Best practice:** Periodically conduct a trend analysis of the types of expenses being claimed by those employees who appear to be at higher risk of abusing the company's T&E policy. This analysis can extend to a review of receipt copies being used across multiple expense reports, as well as a review of sequential receipt numbers across multiple expense reports (which indicates that an employee purchased a block of receipts and is using them to fraudulently claim fake expenses).

Spend Management

It can be useful to periodically aggregate the expenditure information in submitted expense reports by the largest suppliers. By doing so, it may be possible to identify a few suppliers who are receiving the bulk of the company's T&E expenditures. This information can be used to strike volume discount deals with the indicated suppliers. This approach goes over well with employees, since the volume discounts are being arranged with those suppliers that employees are already accustomed to using. When these deals are struck, be sure to include the favored vendors in the corporate T&E policy, indicating that employees should use them.

Dealing with Employee Departures

Many accounting systems require that employees be set up as suppliers in the vendor master file in order to process their expense report reimbursements. If so, periodically set these records to inactive status for any employees who have left the company. This prevents the accounting system from making additional payments to them.

If a company uses an on-line form and automated back end to process expense reports, it should set employees to inactive status in this system once they have left the company. Doing so prevents the system from letting them submit additional expenses for reimbursement.

Expense Report Audits

It is very time-consuming to review every reimbursement request on an employee expense report, as well as all attached receipts. The work is not cost-effective, since most employees are always in compliance with a company's T&E policy. Therefore, a good alternative is to review expense reports on a more limited basis, while requiring a more intensive level of review for the expense reports submitted by those employees who have had compliance problems with the T&E policy in the past. An example of how this approach can be used is:

- No audits for expense reports totaling less than $100.
- Of the expense reports totaling $100 to $1,000, conduct a complete review of ___% of the submitted reports.
- Of the expense reports totaling $1,001 or more, conduct a complete review of a higher percentage of the submitted reports.
- When a serious policy violation is found, flag the submitting individual for a retroactive review of all prior expense reports submitted in the past year.
- Conduct a complete review of the expense reports submitted by the senior management team (mostly to serve notice to the rest of the company that the management team is serious about T&E policy compliance).

Best practice: Adopt a standard policy for selecting expense reports to audit that focuses attention on the high-risk and highest-dollar expense reports.

When an expense report is selected for review, consider engaging in a detailed analysis that includes the following actions:

- *Boarding passes*. Verify that an airline boarding pass is included in the receipts. This is better evidence than a payment receipt, since an employee could have purchased a flight and then cancelled it for a refund.
- *Course grades*. Verify that an official grading document was submitted for a course taken by an employee. As was the case for a boarding pass, an employee could have obtained a receipt for a course and then cancelled it for a refund.
- *Group payments*. If an employee submits a receipt for a payment that was made for a group of employees (such as for a group dinner), check the expense reports of the other employees in that group to see if they also submitted receipts. If so, someone is fraudulently claiming a duplicate reimbursement.
- *Similar dates*. If there are several receipts submitted from the same store, see if they have similar dates and times stamped on them. If so, it could mean that an employee collected receipts from other shoppers exiting the store at the same time.

- *Excessive miles*. Given the high mileage reimbursement rate, someone might take advantage of the situation by reporting an excessive number of miles. When there seems to be a clear overage, use an Internet search engine to estimate the miles that should have been driven, and point out the issue to the employee.
- *Actual receipts*. Many expense reporting systems allow employees to submit scanned copies of their expense receipts. If so, consider adding a requirement that they retain the original receipts for a few months following the expense report date, so that you can request to see the originals. This may reveal that some of the receipts were doctored to show larger expense amounts.
- *Sequential receipt numbers*. An employee may have purchased a block of blank receipts from an office supply store and is using them to create fake receipts for fraudulent claims. If so, the receipts may be consecutively numbered, so look for the numbering across several consecutive expense reports.

If it appears that a claimed expense reimbursement has dubious receipts associated with it, then refuse reimbursement until the employee forwards his credit card statements for the related periods. If the auditor cannot trace the original payments to the credit card statement, then do not issue a reimbursement payment. Of course, this approach only works if the company mandates that *all* payments be made with employee credit cards, rather than with cash.

What if you request to see the original receipt and the employee does not have it? Do not automatically assume that someone is hiding nefarious deeds – it is quite likely that they simply threw it away or lost it. However, make a note of the incident, and if repeated requests result in the same answer, it may be time to engage in a more detailed examination of that person's submissions.

The Escalation Process

A reasonable way to deal with expense report problems is to assume that the first issue was an honest mistake, and so should be dealt with as an educational opportunity regarding how to fill out an expense report form. The employee is presented with that segment of the corporate policy relating to the issue, the nature of the problem is discussed, and the matter is closed. However, this approach should only be used once. If additional problems arise, the presumption changes – we now suspect that the person is trying to go around company rules, so the response shifts away from education and towards a more aggressive response. Possibilities include the issuance of a warning, notification of the person's supervisor and the human resources department, and a notice to the internal auditing department to conduct a detailed review of the person's expense reports for the past few years. After this warning phase, the next step can be termination for the repeated violation of company policies. The trigger for termination will vary, depending on the nature and severity of the offense, but it should not be delayed too long. Once a serial offender has been spotted, it is best to terminate his or her employment and search for a more ethical replacement.

Training for First-Level Supervisors

First-level supervisors are the first line of defense for expense report reimbursements. They are supposed to review and approve employee expense reports, because they know which expenses are warranted and which ones are not. For example, they can tell if an expensive airfare was needed in order to get a senior salesperson in front of a key customer at the last minute in order to secure a major contract. The payables staff does not have this knowledge, and so constitutes a weaker form of review.

Given the importance of supervisory reviews, the company controller should conduct a training session for all new supervisors to go over their review and approval responsibilities. This training should include a discussion of specific fraud cases that have already occurred, as well as what excessive T&E expenses do to company profits and their own bonuses. Further, whenever cases arise in which a supervisor is clearly not being attentive to the submitted expense reports, the chief financial officer (CFO) may need to become involved, to emphasize the importance of these reviews.

When supervisors repeatedly shirk their duties in this area, it needs to be noted in their performance reviews, which in turn impacts their compensation and prospects for promotion. However, adequate and consistent messaging through a repetitive training program should keep these negative performance issues to a minimum.

A Note Regarding Senior Management

As a general rule, try to avoid involving senior management in matters relating to expense reports, on the grounds that most of these issues involve expenditure levels that are more appropriately dealt with at the level of lower to middle levels of management. However, this is not the case when there is evidence of expense report fraud by lower levels of management, since the only people who can deal with this matter are members of *senior* management. Also, if there are quite substantial amounts of expense report fraud by anyone in the organization, then the problem needs to be brought to senior management, since the matter is now material enough to impact the financial results of the corporation.

This recommendation does not mean that T&E policy violations are actively hidden from senior managers. On the contrary, the CFO or the vice president of human resources may have an active interest in these matters, since they involve possible control breaches (a CFO matter) and the possible termination of employment (a human resources matter) for the offending employees.

A Note Regarding Bureaucracy

A key problem when dealing with employees is their ongoing complaints that there is too much bureaucracy associated with expense reports. They are right. It can take a substantial amount of time to assemble the necessary documentation from a business trip, fill out an expense report, and then tussle with the payables staff over whether the form has been completed correctly and all expenses are reasonable. This represents a balance between imposing enough controls to minimize fraud losses and keeping the amount of employee effort to a minimum. There is no easy answer to this balance, but one option is to pin the blame on the Internal Revenue Service, which has quite specific guidelines for expense documentation – which a business must follow. The standard argument can be that the company is merely following the mandates of the government. Those mandates are noted in the following table, which is extracted from IRS Publication 463, *Travel, Gift, and Car Expenses*.

IRS Documentation Requirements

If you have expenses for…	Then you must keep records that show details of the following elements…			
	Amount	Time	Place or Description	Business Purpose
Travel	Cost of each separate expense for travel, lodging, and meals. Incidental expenses may be totaled in reasonable categories such as taxis, fees and tips, etc.	Dates you left and returned for each trip and the number of days spent on business.	Destination or area of your travel (name of city, town, or other designation).	Business purposes for the expense or the business benefit gained or expected to be gained.
Gifts	Cost of the gift.	Date of the gift.	Description of the gift.	--
Transporta-tion	Cost of each separate expense. For car expenses, the cost of the car and any improvements, the date you started using it for business, the mileage for each business use, and the total miles for the year.	Date of the expense. For car expenses, the date of use of the car.	Your business destination.	Business purpose for the expense.

It is especially important to follow the IRS guidelines in order to have an accountable plan. An *accountable plan* follows the IRS regulations for reimbursing employees for business expenses in which reimbursement is not counted as income. This means that reimbursements are not subject to withholding taxes or Form W-2 reporting.

To be an accountable plan, an organization's reimbursement arrangement must include all of the following rules:

- Reimbursed expenses must have a business connection, so that employees have paid or incurred deductible expenses while performing services for the firm.
- Employees must adequately account to the employer for these expenses within a reasonable period of time.
- Employees must return any excess reimbursement to the employer within a reasonable period of time.

The Travel and Entertainment Policy

In essence, the corporate T&E policy tells employees which expenses will and will not be reimbursed. The policy also gives guidelines regarding acceptable expenditures. Sample topics for a T&E policy include the following:

Travel preferences

- States the names of any preferred hotel chains, airlines, and car rental agencies. The company may have bulk purchase discount deals with certain suppliers, so the more volume it can generate with them, the larger the resulting discounts will be.

Expense types

- Describes which expenses will be reimbursed. This section typically includes a discussion of the types of travel arrangements that are considered acceptable, such as:
  - Fly economy for flights having a duration of no more than four hours
  - Fly business class when the trip duration is more than four hours
  - Car rentals must be for intermediate-sized sedans or smaller
  - Hotel rooms cannot be suites
- Notes which expenses will not be reimbursed. This can be a lengthy list, likely including the items in the earlier sample list of non-reimbursement items.

Best practice: If certain types of expenditures are prohibited, this will impact the type of purchase receipt evidence to be submitted. For example, if in-room movies are not reimbursed, then employees will need to submit a complete hotel bill itemization. Similarly, if alcoholic drinks are not reimbursed, employees will need to submit complete restaurant bill itemizations.

Evidence

- States when receipts are required. For example, a receipt may be required for all expenditures over $25.
- Describes which documentation to submit. This may include a statement that the most recent expense report form must be submitted, with all relevant receipts attached.

Approvals

- Notes the levels of approval needed prior to submitting a reimbursement request. For example, a minimal reimbursement request may require no approval at all, while all other expense reports must first be signed by the department manager whose budget will be impacted by the reimbursement request.

Direct company payments

- Describes which expenses are to be directly purchased by the company. Some organizations want to pay directly for all airfare and hotel arrangements, thereby greatly reducing the amounts needing to be reimbursed through expense reports. This also gives the company additional control over the more expensive purchases.

- Describes who gets to use mileage points. Employees are usually allowed to retain the mileage points associated with any airfare that they purchase directly. If the company buys the airfare, the points accrue to the business instead.

The T&E policy will be more closely adhered to if management clearly supports it. This means that senior managers are *not* seen flying first class in clear contravention of the policy, nor are they claiming reimbursement for country club memberships that are also prohibited. When such behavior occurs, expect other employees to follow suit and claim reimbursement for items that are clearly out of compliance with the policy.

Additional T&E Policies

There are several supplemental accounting policies that could be included in the corporate T&E policy, which are intended to provide more structure to what is (and is not) allowed, and to set guidelines for the operation of the payables department. These policies are:

- *Commuting mileage will not be reimbursed.* This policy is fairly obvious, but is needed for those rare cases where an employee persists in attempting to be reimbursed for commuting to and from work.
- *All cash payments must be justified with a receipt.* This policy is intended to close one of the worst loopholes in the expense report system, which is reimbursing people for cash payments that may never have happened.
- *Employees will be reimbursed within __ days of expense report submission.* The number of days until payment should be quite short, since employees may need the cash to pay their credit card statements. This policy is designed to force the payables staff to make rapid payments.

In addition, there should be a policy related to meals. Management needs to make a decision about reimbursing the entire amount of meals or reimbursing on a per diem basis. Either approach works, though the sales staff is more likely to take clients out for meals, and so will not be able to work within the restrictions of a per diem system. The advantages and disadvantages of the two approaches are:

- *Per diem.* This reduces the paperwork included in an expense report. Also, it tends to force employees to purchase less expensive meals. There may be some gaming of the system, where employees purchase very inexpensive meals that cost less than the per diem, and pocket the difference.
- *Reimbursement.* There is more paperwork included in expense reports, but this is essentially a required method when taking business partners out for meals. A few employees will take advantage of this approach to buy inordinately expensive meals.

T&E Policy Updates

Over time, the payables staff will undoubtedly run into recurring issues with employees who disagree with certain aspects of the T&E policy. For example, they may object to a policy where the company does not reimburse for liquor purchases during a meal, or will not allow employees to upgrade to business class seats for long international trips. It can make sense for the payables manager or controller to schedule an annual meeting with senior management to go over these complaints, and relay to them the specific complaints being received. Senior management can then decide whether the policy needs to be changed. Whatever those changes may be, the payables staff is responsible for ensuring that the organization understands them, and must then enforce the changes as written.

> **Best practice:** Update the standard reporting template once a year with the new mileage reimbursement rate, as well as any other information (such as reporting guidelines) that the company wishes to change on the form.

Summary

The vast majority of employees are totally honest, and may even underreport their expense report submissions. However, you will occasionally find an employee who stretches or violates the rules. Once found, this person's expense reports should *always* be examined, as well as all of his or her prior submissions. Thus, the rule for expense report examinations is to audit them, with 100% reviews for any violators found. This is a highly cost-effective way to focus attention on those areas most likely to result in expense savings.

The intelligent use of expense report audits should contribute to a gradual decline in the amount of time spent reviewing expense reports. The audits will likely begin by encompassing most expense reports, because some managers are concerned about the potential loss of funds through non-compliant behavior. Then, when the auditing approach is tailored to watch for higher-risk expenditures, managers will likely become more comfortable with the concept of reviewing a smaller percentage of expense reports.

Glossary

A

Accountable plan. A plan that follows the IRS regulations for reimbursing employees for business expenses in which reimbursement is not counted as income.

E

Expense report. A form used to track spending on behalf of a business.

P

Per diem. An allowance or payment made for each day.

Index

Accountable plan.................................. 13

Card misuse 5
Cash advances 6
Commuting mileage policy 15

Documentation 7

Employee records.................................. 9
Employee reimbursement policy 15
Escalation process 11
Excessive tipping................................... 5
Expense report auditing........................ 10

Illegible receipts 3
IRS documentation requirements 13

Late submissions 4

Mileage analysis.....................................11
Mileage overstatements...........................5
Missing receipts 3

Non-reimbursement items.......................1

On-line expense reporting.......................7

Per diem reimbursement 15
Policy update frequency.........................16

Receipt numbering analysis 11

Senior management involvement..........12
Spend management 9
Supervisor training.................................12

Travel and entertainment policy............13